DANCING
IN THE FLAME

DANCING IN THE FLAME

Valerie Denton

with illustrations by Clare Williams

◇

THE DIAMOND PRESS

First published by Diamond Press, 1991
5 Berners Mansions, 34–6, Berners Street, London W1.

Copyright © Valerie Denton, 1991
All rights reserved

Printed by Whitstable Litho Ltd, Kent.
Typeset by Roger Booth Associates, Newcastle upon Tyne.

ISBN 0 948684 15 4

Dedicated to all those who dare to dance and to all those who have helped me to.

"We dance round in a ring and suppose
But the Secret sits in the middle and knows."
Robert Frost

"You have three wings:
The first unfolds aloft in the highest height
The second dips its way dripping sweat on the earth.
Over, under, and through all things whirls the third."
Hildegard of Bingen

CONTENTS

I

Dream Horse (illustration) 2
Dream Horse 3
North and South (illustration) 4
North and South 5
That Day 6
The Poem is just the Beginning 7
The Task 9
Divine Inspiration 12
Circle Dance 13
Incense (illustration) 14
Incense 15
Dancing Women 16
The Comforter 17
Parallel Lines 18

II

High Flying Bird (illustration) 20
High Flying Bird 21
Ladywell 23
Sienna (illustration) 24
Sienna 25
Moths in the Night (illustration) ... 26
Moths in the Night 27
In the Garden (illustration) 28
In the Garden 29
Spring Rose 30

Two Poems for Music 32
Snow at Easter 33
Mountain and Fjord (illustration) 34
Mountain and Fjord 35
Munch's Women 36
Blood Loss 37
Badingham 1990 39
Magdalen 40
Hot Stuff 41
Sweet Breath 42
Blowing up a Storm 43
The Dorn Path 44

III
Iona (illustration) 46
Iona 47

I

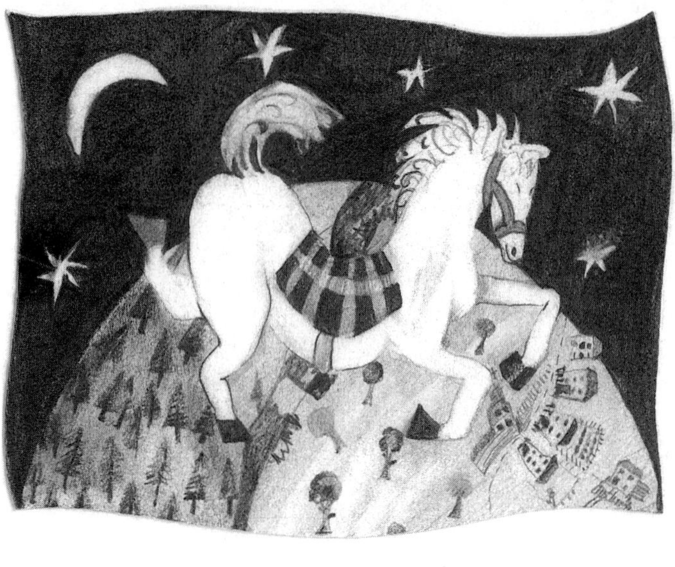

DREAM HORSE

Last night I rode my dream horse,
He was white with a golden mane.
I forgot my fear of riding,
Or of danger, as I held the rein.

We soared over moonlit hedges,
Delved into night-clothed woods.
I gasped at the effort of the race,
Exhilarated by the ease when we rode.

I patted my steed to coax him,
He knew every touch and tone,
And did just what I wanted –
We seemed to act as one.

The night began to take our heat,
I felt him tremble and tire;
So I wrapped him up in morning mist,
And I called to the sun for fire.

He drifted away in the clouds of my dreams –
I could still feel him gently move.
But I woke in the raw, still light of dawn,
And I turned to you, my love.

I often think where my dream horse went,
Perhaps he's roaming free.
I'd like him here in my dream of life
To stay with my love and me.

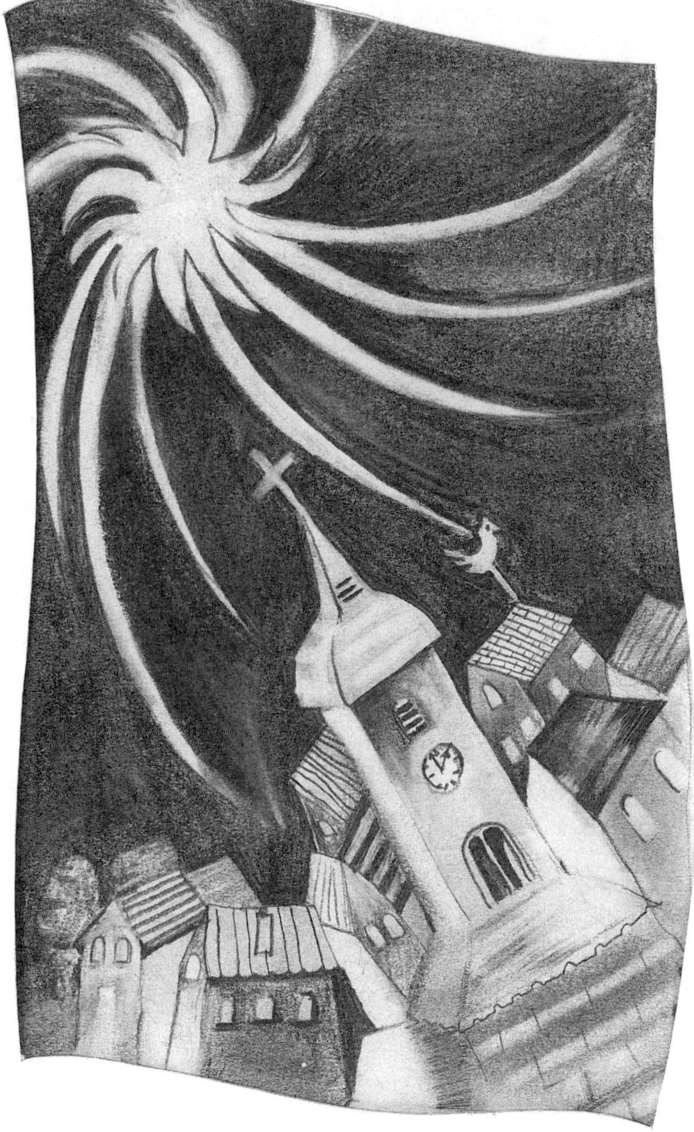

NORTH AND SOUTH

If you've ever seen the sun pouring its gold over smoke,
Gilding the greyest towers and spires,
Transforming bleak horizons into glistening tiaras;
You will know how I feel when the rooftops of London
Come into view, like a badly fitting jig-saw.
Looking forward, looking back, there's no light here for me.

Sometimes, in my dreams, I see the sun,
Showing its face, like a pretty child, to all,
Not caring if some people prefer the dark.
But that is not our sun, the one that comes with us,
Who tries so hard, but who's
Beaten back by night,
Knowing that the soft of evening should not be spent alone.

And, not wanting to separately shine on you and me,
He sinks and sulks in a corner of the sky.
He must possess and be possessed by that which is his own.
So he waits like a rich-robed god for our coming together again.
Meanwhile, the sun cries rain,
And the gentle evening runs from the lonely night.

THAT DAY

That day was green – the earth became my sky.
I looked away from space that man was busy conquering
And looked to find my own discovery.
He sat criss-crossed with lush green strands of grass,
His hair like Autumn corn, and I felt bound,
As if by spiders' threads; sensed soft, warm earth
Against my skin; I wanted all
Of nature's realm within myself.

From this great glory of life,
I turned to natural wonders.
A whole new world was waiting there
In those green eyes that looked
And loved what they could see.
The sun was in his face,
The warmth of summer in his form.
He was part of earth and yet, my earth.
I'd never had a part of nature for myself.
We picked some flowers, brilliant shapes,
Reflected in the lake.
I felt a child again, happy to hold
A part of life inside.

I took my pen and wrote in simple words,
Like a child soft from sleep.
The letters form, the flowers distract,
"For our wedding," he had said.
But I am joined already,
In body and in mind.
I had made my pact with the world outside,
Had learned to love it,
And he had made the bond.
I'll walk with him,
Whatever colour day.

THE POEM IS JUST THE BEGINNING

"And, at the end, the poets stood up –
They looked just like ordinary people."
That's what she said, this person
Who didn't know that I couldn't say
That sometimes I try to be one.
But, even as I go to write the word,
I still can't actually say it.
"Poet...poetic...poetical... what on earth do they mean?"
A writer lives with his dreams, that is all I know.
With those come his loves, his fears, his heavens and hells,
His deaths and births – karmic regurgitation.
Again and again, and on and on, willing the process,
Whatever it is, to stop, just for a while;
So the body, the mind, the soul, and whatever
Part has been over-used, to rest,
And purge itself of excessive overload.
That hope is as far away as the latest poem,
Or only as near as the next.

Because, if the simple truth were told, poets,
If asked to do so, may be unable to stand;
Drunk, giddy, or high, whatever the stop-gap is;
Or suddenly struck dumb, having a silent night,
When it's safer to stay inside, it seems,
Even if it is in the recesses of the mind.
And if poets drink, or take whatever they can get,
It's because they sweat and cry and curse a lot,
Make maddening love to highest heaven.

For God's sake, if I could stand on any night,
I wouldn't wave this flimsy bit of stuff around;
I'd fix your eyes to mine and zoom to where you are.
You might go home and say, "I met a poet tonight,
She didn't speak, just looked, she seemed in a dream to me."
And, there, you've said it better than I could ever write.
Somewhere between the waking and the sleeping state
Is where we're best to be.

This hand that writes has the urge to heal,
Touch type for people's hope.
It reaches for another hand and finds it,
Extraordinarily – the same.

THE TASK

Isis on the water, searching frantically;
Her face a stream of tears.
Where was he – Osiris?
Anywhere and everywhere.
Could she find him, flood him with her love?
Be both haven and an ark?
Lay his shattered body out,
Warm him with her pungent oils,
Caress and gently press
The life-force into him?

But she hadn't seen the casket –
Was it a coffin or a crib?
She had bent her body over it
So many times in dreams.
So many times she'd put out hands
To touch, and only felt the cold
Hard stone, the glass, the wood
Beneath her healing hands.

On flowed the tide of the ceaseless Nile –
Back came hollow emptiness.
Until she saw the tree bent
Low over fertile banks;
Heather, purple, wild and free
Growing thick in every crack.
A hiding-place and signal post.
She went, she saw, she wept.
A casket embedded in a tree,
With irises for funeral flowers.
And all around, the moaning marsh;
The mist and tears, a veil
Covering her face.

But, returning to her family,
She lost her crown of light
For horns, a crescent –
Cow-like she became.
Some expected anger, some distress.
She could only give out love,
Her family's passions spent.

No baby in a basket, this,
But God entombed in a casket.
Pushed out, not to save,
But to destroy.
She'd finally found the broken man –
Only pieces to mourn and kiss.

Another fragmented search,
Needing the light of the moon.
Her task? to make him whole again,
Albeit an image of the man.
She magicked into being
The vital, missing part.
She held it high, she brought it low,
Into herself, to revitalise,
To procreate for earth.
And now, instead of tears,
Her milk flowed warm and free.
In its elemental form, the love
Gushed out, was taken and used up,
And from this made a suckling babe again,
Destroying the god in him.

Isis could love, Isis could save.
Isis could cry, Isis could have.
Osiris was loved, Osiris was saved,
But when he cried, what did he have?

The fertile river took them to its heart.
It floated them away from the pain of their past lives.
It took them wider, further on, until they couldn't stop.
It left them finally on peaceful shores
To find and love themselves.

Isis and Osiris, goddess and god again;
Eternal lovers or a phallic ritual?
Isis in you, Osiris in me.
The moon in you, the sun in me.

The empty sky with the lightness of a bird.
Deep underworlds, dark with a sad soul's night.
Breaking down, breaking open, breaking up.
Osiris is you, Isis is me.
We are floating drifting,
And free... free.

DIVINE INSPIRATION

The door slammed shut. He'd gone.
"Good riddance," the child in me said.
A pause, a momentary drift.
The door stayed shut. She had come.
She seemed to be looking after him.
"What him? Love him?" I said.
"Please, choose another one.
Pig-headed at the very least, that one,
And, anyway, I hate him."

She stood her ground behind his chair.
She seemed resigned and somehow sad.
Not me, I wanted out,
To hide, not seek, to run.
"So what must I do?" I idly asked,
"Use my own devices, like
Cry, or rant and rave?"
I thought she said, I thought it was,
"Just love and let him be."

I opened the door. They'd gone.
Alone in the hall, the emptiness jarred,
But I felt compelled to
Become the irrepressible,
Give love and anger back.
With this divinity, came sanity,
In giving out, a giving up.
My chair now next to his,
The him to her combined.

She's standing now between us both,
Her arms outstretched like this.
She's hovering now and rising slowly,
Slowly rising – with healing in her wings.

CIRCLE DANCE

Round we go in the circle dance,
          Inner circle out,
          Outer circle in.
Gather motion now to start,
          Fast go one way,
          Slow, the next.

As I spin inside the
Man-made world,
Turning myself out,
Inside out to
Face the self-born world.
          Stand stock still,
          Confront myself,
          Partnering for life,
          Formation, sequence made.

Round we go in the circle dance,
          Round and round,
          And side to side.
When do we ever stop?

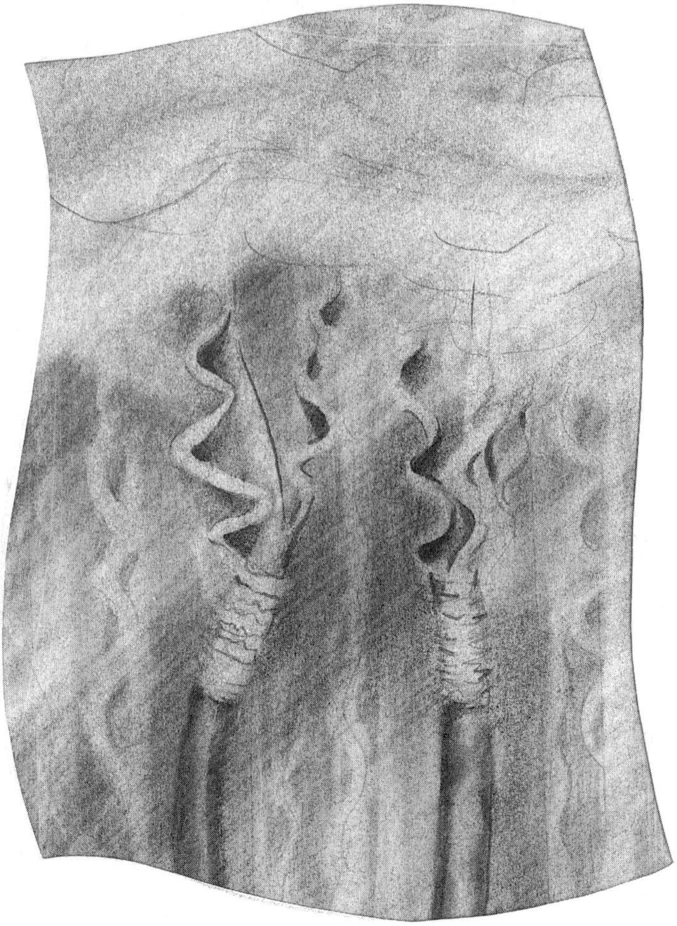

INCENSE

I am incensed.
Burning embers
Smoulder red,
Twisting wraithe-like
Up into your
Tallest heights.
Then, swirling
Round, disperse,
Enveloping us
In perfumed haze.

When the glow is
Gone, and only
Scented ash
Is left,
I, heady with
The choking smell,
Stand tall and straight,
To meet you
Burning there,
And ask…
"Do we keep the glow
Deep down inside of us,
Settle for fragrant ease,
Or, do we go up in smoke?"

DANCING WOMEN

Dancing woman in white,
Gliding on the stage or
Dancing in the square where
You were savagely knocked down.

        Whirling for joy, and free,
        Seconds before the shots and
        Screams mingled with the
        Trundling of tanks.

When women from Armenia or Georgia move,
Graceful, ghost-like, veiled in white –
Her spirit calms and hushes us – though
Heavy with grief, she's light as air.

        Dressed suitably for wedding or for funeral,
        They perform beyond their states.
        Their heavy skirts encircle broken earth;
        Their feet and hands can carry us away.

Mourning women in black,
Holding candles in the dark;
Pictures of loved ones, bedraggled red flowers –
Joining hands, they slowly dance again.

THE COMFORTER

The comforter has been
Here, kneeling while I wait.
Swaying, dark folds eclipse
The light – deep enough
To bury in.

I daren't look up
At the face – I may be
Dazzled, or else it's dim.
So I ask, as always,
"What must I do?"

She – it could be he –
Her legs are strong as trees,
Lifts her hands apart.
"Is she giving up on me?
No, no, simpler than that."

For me I feel her close,
And then to others, I open
Up this self-sealed trunk
And, throwing out these held-down arms,
Hug the weary one to me.

PARALLEL LINES

In touch again,
Hearing you, I'm
Holding on, we're
Tapping the source,
Exchanging energy.

Reaching out, I'm
Holding up my
Arms, encircling you,
We're head and heart and
Fingertip in touch.

In sight of you again,
My vision's clear, I
Know your face, your
Outstretched hand, we're
Close, it's neck to neck.

Tasting lips on mine –
A knowing kiss, I
Want to know it more –
Me, who never did know how,
Needs knower and the known.

The scents of rose and incense
Now combine, I
Give the jasmine, then,
To you, who seems to be the one.

Choosing then, choosing now –
A past and future present.

II

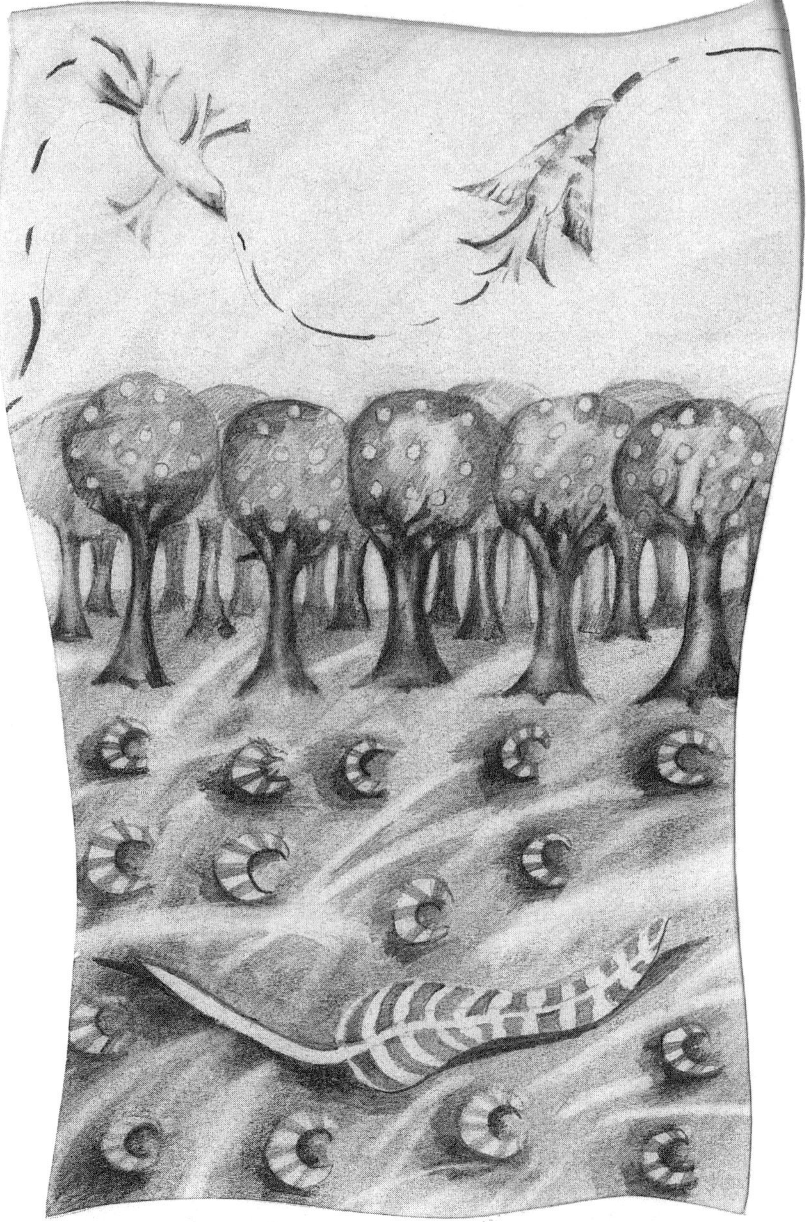

HIGH FLYING BIRD

For Jay

I walk, you talk.
I talk, you walk and
Suddenly, we stop.
We listen, look.
I pick a feather up –
That jazzy bird again.

Woods I've walked in,
Accompanied and alone –
Listening, looking, still –
The quietness startled by
The screeching of a jay,
That siren of the soul.

I watch him as he
Flits and breaks
The silence up,
Outlining territory,
And always, screeching calls,
Expecting some reply.

Then, heading downwards,
Swaying, tail wings fold,
He rocks, the blue streak
Quivers and, just as
I look up to see his
Launching out – he's gone.

My spirit, soul, is
Soaring now with him,
Circumnavigating trees and
With a sharp intake of breath,
Outwards go, our wings spread wide,
To span the woods and fields and towns.

Gliding, almost hovering,
We feel an upward pull,
And, lifted up, we're
Feathered, nested, warm.
Swooping now, I plummet
Down to earth again.

But you, my glossy,
Deep, dark bird
Have lifted off,
Forever wheeling free.
With every sudden rush of wind,
I, you, we are three.

LADYWELL

Lady well to do,
Lost in your valley of
Streams that sing
With the golden green
Of nightingales.

Lady does do well,
In warm-bricked
Cottage and manor-house,
With sheep in the valley
And shepherds on the hill.

Ladywell gives out
Her clear, cold springs
And gushing streams, tumbling down,
Like hair, waiting to be washed,
Luxuriating skin in warmth.

Lady does me well.
She is becoming me, reflected in the pool
Of her silent, secret place.
I know she's there, resting on the banks,
Hiding beneath primeval plants.

Ladywell, your love is there
Whenever wells spring up
Or streams run clear.
I see your face, your shining hair,
Your turf-like cloak and hands washed clean.

Ladywell has come to me,
Here, in her lush, green fields.
She waits beside the stony banks
And never follows but beckons back.
Return, re-live in Ladywell.

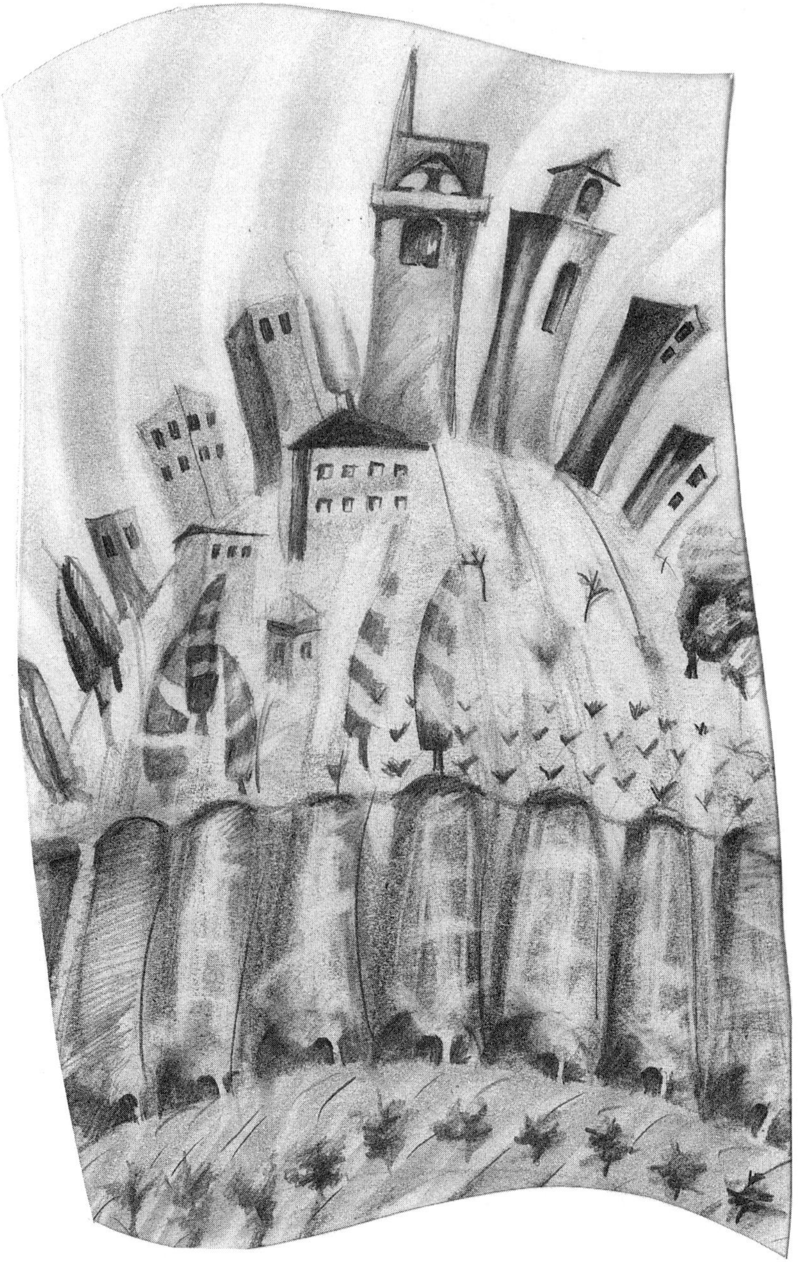

SIENNA

Seven towers reach up
Straight from earthen hills.
As I reach to tip the
Sun at dawn – "With my body I thee honour."

Sunflowers stare vainly,
Massed in cracking fields.
I slowly open out like them
To dry up in the heat – "And he went into the desert."

Lush vineyards line up
Outside the window of my room.
I lose myself in their tangled mass
And purple-staining juice – "Take this in remembrance of me."

Multi-coloured marble and
Pillars striped like rock;
The blue domes crowned with gold;
My head is lifted up and back – "Hail Mary, full of grace."

In the airiness of her basilica
Saint Catherine fills the space.
The woman in me at last can kneel,
Her reverence unwatched – "I believe in the communion of
saints."

Dawn brings its veil
Over the San Gimignano hills.
With a carillon of bells, the
Sun sets slow behind the monastery – "Into this earth I
commend thy soul."

My eyes, reddened like the sky,
Pick out the seven tapers
Blazing in the darkened square
For this feast of a life-time for me – "I baptise you in his name."

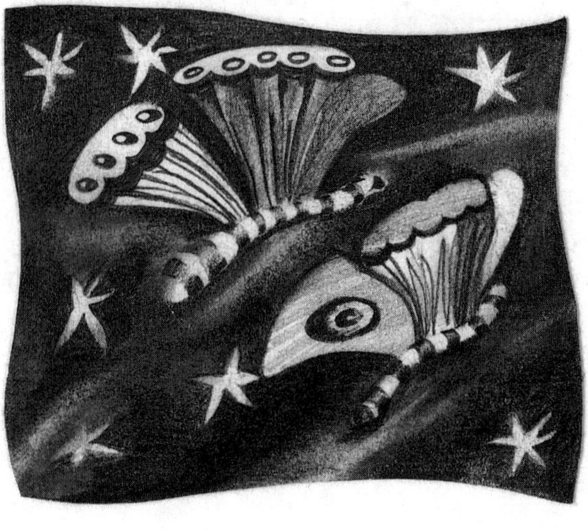

MOTHS IN THE NIGHT

Closer came the whirr of wings,
A rushing hush, as ash falls,
Softly resting now, the longed-for peace
From beating at the light.

Closer I came than I've ever been
To stopping silently and still,
Daring to land and balance wings,
So delicate in flight.

The moment I brushed your face,
Invisible wings took off.
Somewhere a light was turning on,
While I lay poised in the dark.

Peace showered down like flower dust.
Cupping my wings, you let me go,
Out into morning light – for the briefest touch
Means a moth may no longer fly.

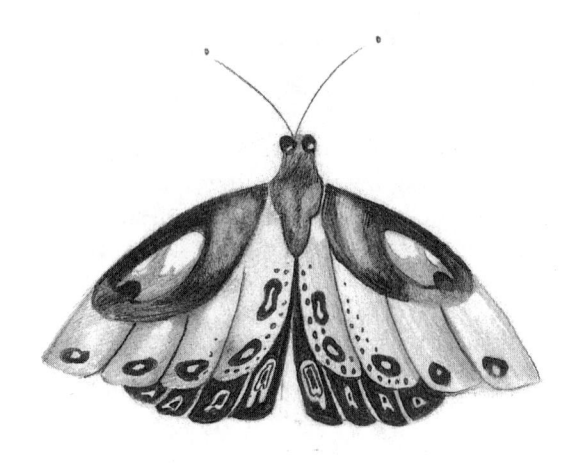

IN THE GARDEN

For J.D.

Motionless, we were
For a moment, as a
Moth settles on a leaf.
Gone the flurry of restless wings –
Here and now, the
Quiet time we two
Spent as one.

Speechless I was
And far away, yet near,
I saw a filmy gauze,
Swirling in the wind and
Patterned by the sun –
The dancing trees and flowered grass –
Yet silence in between,
So close, but
Out of reach.

Fleeting and transient and
Not for us to hold or
Reason out, the
Talk of inner depths
Had passed – just being there,
But only 'just' was,
In the end, enough.

SPRING ROSE

Walking under trees
That suddenly shower blossom,
Reminds me of a walk
We took when snow
Softly shouldered us,
Made us think of May,
Anticipating fulness,
For us, treading on thin ice.

Seeing a familiar tree,
Heavy and white in Spring,
Resembling hoar-frost,
Stiffly coating branches
That suddenly can snap;
My son beside me
Wants only petal pink,
And, finding a rosette
Fallen from an almond tree,
Picks it up and blows
Away the dust – we
Look to make a bunch of these
Roses of Spring for him.

Sifting through the heaps
Like icing sugar flowers,
I think of the fuller rose
That comes in June.
The heady-scented ones – scarlet, pink and white,
Hundreds of roses we'll have to pick
For only a few drops of oil.
But then my house will be always full
Of their tenuous, musky essence.

Perfume-maker, me.
Petal-picker, him,
And one who walks
Glad of the snow in his hair.
We are one and the same,
Sharing these sometimes snowflake,
Sometimes rose-petal showers
That come again and again and again.

TWO POEMS FOR MUSIC

BELLOWS OF FIRE

Bellows,
        blow your life-breath into me.
Bellow
        out your words – celestial food for me.
Bellow
        up the flames from sparks – putting fire in me.
Bellow
        bells, ring out – there still is time for me.

                Below the hills I
                Sit and whisper
                Words that warm the winds
                Into wishes for me.

FLUTE MUSIC

Flute music sounding in my ears,
Caressing me with waves of rippling song.
An echo, distant, plaintive, says
"Play me, play my flute, play me,
Please don't ever stop."

I take the flute gently into my hands,
Mouthing the notes, I bring it low,
Then upwards, soaring into heights and scales unknown;
And slowly, surely, bring it back to rest.
A tune of creation has been played.

SNOW AT EASTER

A solitary cross stands in the snow –
Seasons and times in disarray again.
Death on ice and passion in a blizzard,
Trying to resurrect in sodden robes.

Then the pain that was numbed at first,
Stinging and smarting into life,
Longing for the swaddling robes
And the pungent smell of oil.

But stones roll easily in snow,
More able to be cracked and broken open;
Shattered shards remain on the walk to the grave,
Sealed by ice, star-flowered with frost.

I pick up the pieces and make a cairn of standing stones,
Surrounding them with broken bits of wood,
Light them up, blow to kindle them and
Wait an eternity for the embers to glow.

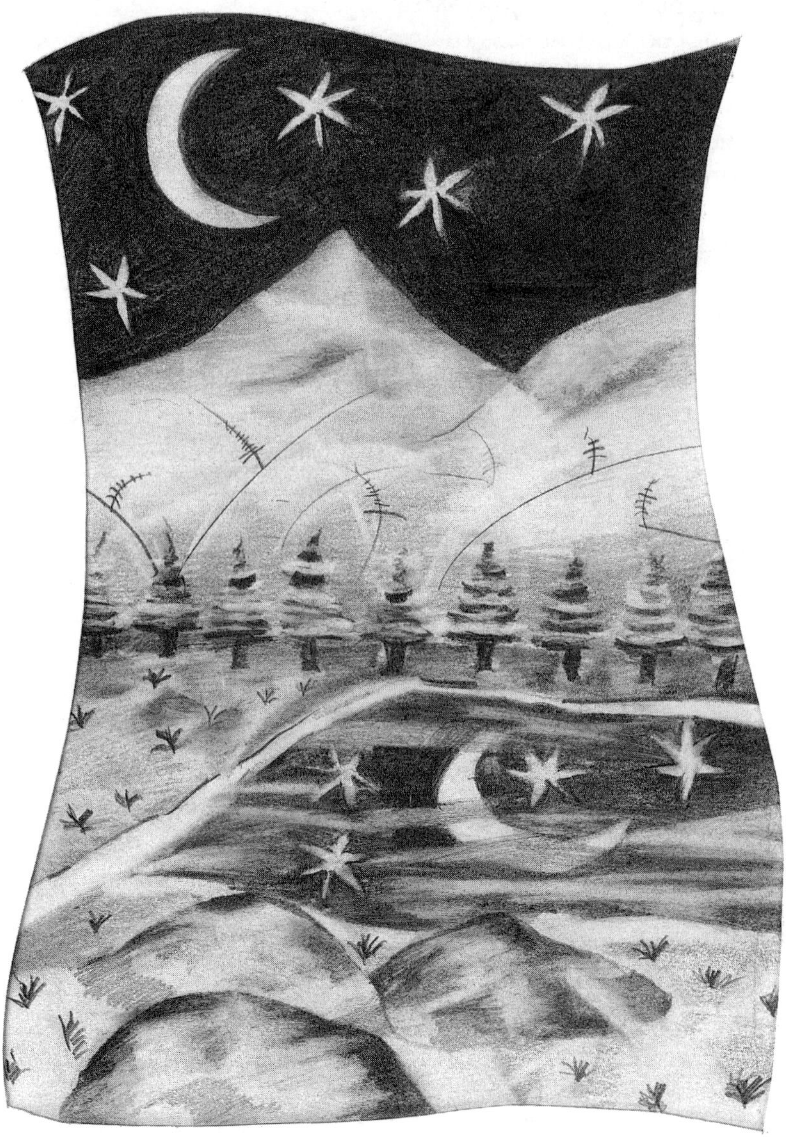

MOUNTAIN AND FJORD

Mountain man, your stone is
A heaven-reaching crag.
Fjord woman – your waters are
As deep as he is high.

The fjord below the rock-face
Takes the seething white force as it falls;
The mountain above the cascading veil
Keeps the power of the peaks in its heights.

Whether green, or blue, or shadowy grey,
She reflects his every mood.
Mists may obscure him, but still she keeps
The memory of him in her depths.

Mountain man, you are
Glacier born, from
Stone reformed, you
Shape her concave image.

She is azure blue when the sun is up,
Or grey-flecked white when the wind
Whips the waves in a
Sudden summer storm.

They are mirror and stone,
A rock and crystal looking-glass.
Without his heights, she could not sink low;
When they embrace, the heights and depths are one.

MUNCH'S WOMEN

Munch painted night scenes
With a moon like an 'I' on the sea.
Three women wait silently on the shore –
One in white, one in red and
One in lingering black.

While watching the moon write italics
On the sea, and punctuate the sky,
I slowly emerge from the shadows,
Black dress rustling like the trees,
Whose colour lightens with dawn.

When Italian skies were dawning for me,
I was the white and delicate one;
Drenched in the redness of their fire,
I was parched, unquenched by a life
Of lassitude in the sun.

Now the Nordic moons are rising for me,
I become the scarlet one,
Waiting for the midnight sun to
Take the mystery from snow, the edge off frost,
And gradually melt the ice.

Munch painted night scenes
With the moon like an 'I' on the sea.
His trio of women now within –
The black one's stalking death,
The white one's heat is full of fire,
The red one's splitting like hot ice.

BLOOD LOSS

After a day of
Blood and pain, and
Desperate for rest, I
Saw the face of a hill.
Not steep, or rock, as
Might confront a climber –
A face had become the hill.

As I blinked, the bushes
Rolled in the wind like
Deep-set eyes, hollow from some
Agony or suffering.
The face began to turn, bend down,
The head lolled low, like a crucifixion scene.
And the eyes kept rolling, and the
Head kept lolling, and I was stuck in a
Moving image I didn't want to watch.

What was he dying for?
Or was it something coming up from me,
Deep-felt, that could only see in the
Landscape its own projected pain?
And I was looking now, hoping
For a stream to course and
Slowly trickle down the
Dust-hot face, to the
Mouth I couldn't see,
Never quite could reach –
Dried-up and cracked like
Worn-out dugs.

I wanted to kiss and spring
Him into life, the tears
Welled up instead, but I was
Separated from so far a
Distance, I felt I'd
Never touch or feel, or
Ever see him living now.

Maybe it was a sign to say
Those rolling hills are furrowed deep;
They're taking the strain and soon,
Like the face, may fade away.
Perhaps it was a silent plea for help.
I heard it – lying at the bottom of the hill.

BADINGHAM, 1990

For T.C.

Surrender, soft and silky white,
Wafted down by air
Heated by the coal fire;
Spitting out sparks as the
Fountain water flows.

                    Drinking silver water
                    With the roses of dawnlight.
                    Tasting firewater in a
                    Crimson, sunset sky.

And, in the languid afternoon,
The sun clears the haze from
An elegant lounge, highlighting
Curves and golden lamps;
Picking out the splashing red
Of a painted, summer flower.

Longings return for
That house of ease,
Where love and laughter mix
Evening drinks of delight.
I savour the warmth and
Its lazy charm,
As winter melts down its icy edge
Into snow-dropped mud.

                    If my longings are there,
                    Then I am too.
                    At the source of desire,
                    The shadow of a thought
                    Makes a mansion in my mind,
                    And room upon heavenly room.

MAGDALEN

She will be his magdalen
And keep the garden bright.
She will be his caring guard
To see him through the night.

Martha's in the kitchen but
She stays there at his feet;
Pouring oil on transforming pain
So they can wholly meet.

She will be his magdalen.
When he's risen, what does she do?
Wait in the garden, prepare the balm,
In everyone's passion see – you.

HOT STUFF

So I said to Martha,
"If cooking's what you're best at,
Do it then.
No good mooning around like Mary,
Devoted though she is."
And she said to me, "Some people
Say I'm always in the kitchen,
Subservient-like."
So I said to her, "You prepare,
You cook and then you have to serve."

You should see them together,
Those two now – one without the other
Just doesn't work.
Well, I mean, you can't contemplate
Your life away – you need a little action
Now and then.
Then Martha said, "I always stir it up."
Then Mary said, "I get to the heart of things."
Then Martha said, "The quickest way is through the stomach."
Then Mary said, "Eat your heart out then."

So I said to Mary,
"If you do have to wash the master's feet,
Couldn't you clean the floor a bit?"
Then I said to Martha,
"Stop flapping around with recipes,
And sit down for a bit."
If Mary was half a Martha and
She was the other half,
They'd make a woman yet.

SWEET BREATH

And the sweet breath of heaven
Came down upon my face.
The trace of a touch
Around nose and eye;
A lifting slight of lips;
A flutter of eyelash on the cheeks;
A feather-down wisp of hair.

Was it me or the wind that moaned?
A long, soft moan, gently exhaling
Precious, sweet and honeyed breath;
A fanning of a flame so small,
Bowing and flickering in the breeze,
That cooled to dew on a
Face flushed into life.

BLOWING UP A STORM

In the eye of the storm
   Is a central stillness
That settles the restlessness
   Of our mind's eye.

Wandering in the storm
    Causes the soul to cease
All action, wait, become still,
    Shelter till calmness comes again.

When the wind abates that
    Has hushed all other noise,
Whirlwinds and hurricanes become
    The winds of change in us.

THE DORN PATH

Dunblane to Bridge of Allan

Let the river say it –
"Inner chatter, be still."
Let the tree trunk feel it –
"You can and you will."

Let the pathway take you –
"Follow, not lead on."
Let the journey quieten you –
"Your troubles will be gone."

Waterfalls, streams and the river-side;
Trees bending low, the silent rocks that rest –
They are inside and outside and always beside
You, who are earth, air, fire and water blessed.

III

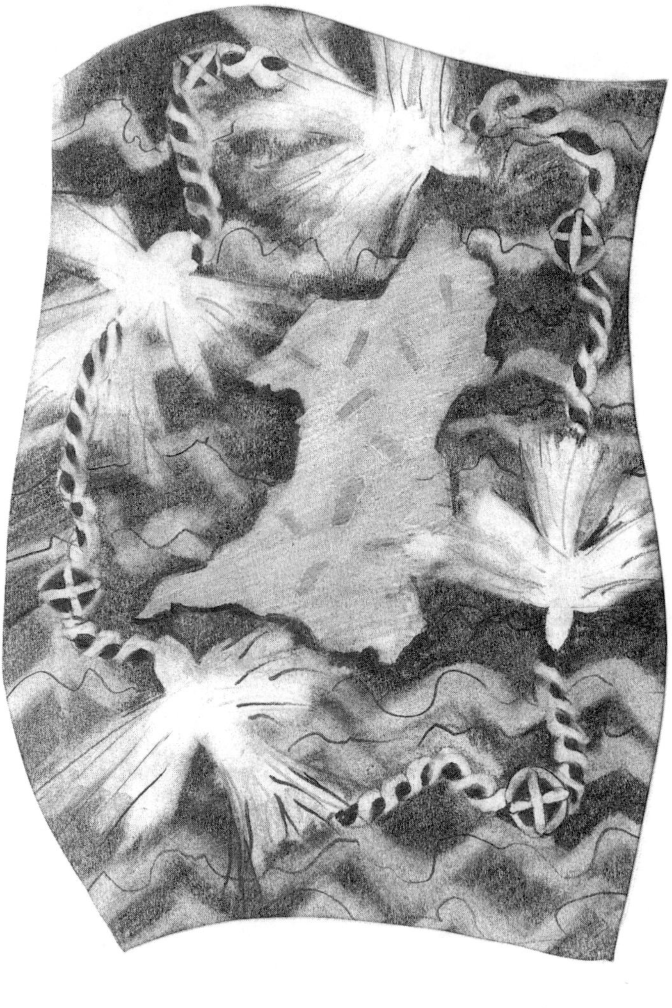

IONA

Iona –
Thin line
Between matter
And spirit.
Enter in
That sacred isle –
You will be
Changed beyond
Your wildest
Dreams.

Iona is
A dream –
Wild and
Yet, contained.
Walk upon
Her shores and
You will find
The fury that
Comes with peace,
Beforehand unobtained.

Iona.
I'll be there again soon.
For she alone knows that
No-one can say "Iona"
Without becoming
Still, remembering
The white-bleached sand,
The squally showers,
The turquoise sea and
Warm, pink rocks.

Iona.
I do not
Own her.
She is yours and
Mine and everyone's,
Coming to us,
Like her dove
Across the water,
Winging the sound –
I–O–N–A.

Photograph by Mark Brookes.

Acknowledgements

'In the Garden' has been published in the newsletter 'Archangel' edited by Simon Miles

'Dream Horse' has been set to music for a twenty part choir by Rosemary Duxbury.

I should like to thank the following friends for their help and encouragement:

Jay Ramsay for editing help, Carole Bruce for her caring support, John Darby for help with administration and distribution, Peter Mobbs for family help, Briar Maxwell for valued dance tuition and all contributors, advance subscribers and supporters.

The Diamond Press is also publishing a pamphlet series. The first five titles are: Ark – Eric Ratcliffe; Exquisite Salmon Wish – Helen White; Paeonies – Richard Wainwright; The Rain, The Rain – Jay Ramsay; and Towards Dawn – Jenny Johnson. All are priced @ £3 inclusive of p&p.

For information on Jay Ramsay's CHRYSALIS – THE POET IN YOU, please send an sae to The Secretary, 38 Lee Road, Lynton, North Devon, or telephone 0598–53440.

This includes Parts I and II by post, editing, one-to-one sessions and the workshop 'The Sacred Space of the Word' held regularly around the UK.

Other titles available from Diamond Press

PSYCHIC POETRY – A MANIFESTO – Jay Ramsay. 72pp. p/b. £3.25.

JOURNEY TO THE EDGE OF LIGHT – SELECTED POEMS 1965–1985 – Geoffrey Godbert. 86pp. p/b, with illustrations and photographs. £4.50.

FIRST THINGS – POEMS 1971–1987 – Lizzie Spring. 81pp. p/b, illustrated with line drawings by the author and full cover painting. £4.75.

THE GREAT RETURN:

THE OPENING/KNIFE IN THE LIGHT – A STAGE-POEM/THE HOLE (the first three books) – Jay Ramsay. 226pp. p/b, illustrated with sheet music and collage.£7.95.

IN THE VALLEY OF THE SHADOW – A CINE-POEM-CUM-FANTASY/DIVINATIONS (bks 4–5) – Jay Ramsay. 379 pp. p/b, with a portrait by Carole Bruce and tinted page graduations. £9.95. (The Diamond Press 2 vol. Standard Edition: £14.95 for a set)

SEA OF GLASS – SELECTED POEMS 1972–1989 – Diana Durham. 148pp. p/b, with drawings by Catherine Smedley. £5.95.

INTERPRETING THE TREE – Carolyn Askar. 91pp. p/b, with line drawings by Lizzie Spring. £4.95.

FOR NOW – Geoffrey Godbert & Jay Ramsay. 111pp. p/b, with photographs by Carole Bruce and portrait sketches by Jenny Fry and Elizabeth McKane.£5.95.

Cheques to The Diamond Press: 5 Berners Mansions, 34–6 Berners Street, London W1P 3DA (071–580 0767). Telephone orders welcome. Add £1 p&p.

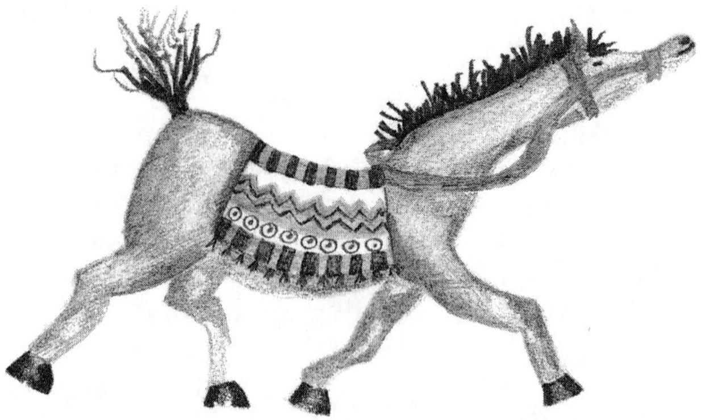